Alex W. Pitzer

Confidence in Christ

Or, faith that saves

Alex W. Pitzer

Confidence in Christ
Or, faith that saves

ISBN/EAN: 9783337314408

Printed in Europe, USA, Canada, Australia, Japan

Cover: Foto ©Lupo / pixelio.de

More available books at **www.hansebooks.com**

CONFIDENCE IN CHRIST;

OR,

FAITH THAT SAVES.

BY

REV. A. W. PITZER, D.D.,

PROFESSOR OF BIBLICAL LITERATURE IN HOWARD UNIVERSITY, WASHINGTON, D. C.; AUTHOR OF "THE NEW LIFE NOT THE HIGHER LIFE," ETC.

"He that believeth not God hath made him a liar, because he believeth not the record that God gave of his Son."—THE APOSTLE JOHN.

PHILADELPHIA:

PRESBYTERIAN BOARD OF PUBLICATION
AND SABBATH-SCHOOL WORK,
No. 1334 CHESTNUT STREET.

INTRODUCTION.

For thirty-and-three years have I trusted Christ as he is revealed in the Holy Scriptures; in all this time he has never in a single instance deceived or disappointed me. He is commended to all men everywhere as One in every way worthy of their most implicit confidence.

That this work may lead the unsaved to trust him, and the saved to trust him more fully, is the prayer of the author.

Washington, D. C., September 14, 1887.

CONTENTS.

SECTION I.
	PAGE
THE IMPORTANCE OF FAITH	7

SECTION II.
WHAT, THEN, IS CONFIDENCE IN CHRIST, OR SAVING FAITH? 15

SECTION III.
FAITH FOUNDED ON EVIDENCE 23

SECTION IV.
THREE VIEWS OF FAITH—THE ROMISH, THE RATIONALISTIC, THE CHRISTIAN 34

SECTION V.
THE TESTIMONY OF GOD 44

SECTION VI.
Faith not a Mere Act, but a Life 55

SECTION VII.
Faith the Differentia of Christian Life . 67

SECTION VIII.
Faith's Warrant is God's Word 73

SECTION IX.
The Assurance of Faith 77

SECTION X.
The Growth of Faith 86

SECTION XI.
The Trials of Faith 93

CONFIDENCE IN CHRIST.

SECTION I.

THE IMPORTANCE OF FAITH.

THE word of God attaches the utmost possible importance to faith, even going so far as to say, "Without faith it is impossible to please him," and "Whatsoever is not of faith is sin."

Jesus of Nazareth, who claimed to be a Teacher sent from God, commanded his servants to proclaim to the world, "He that believeth and is baptized shall be saved; but he that believeth not shall be damned." Nay, even more than this: he said to Nicodemus, "He that believeth not is condemned already, because he hath not believed in the name of the only-begotten Son of God." The apostle John points out the moral necessity for the unbeliever's damnation when he affirms that "he that believeth not God hath made him a liar."

Throughout every portion of the Scriptures the importance of faith is insisted upon with emphasis, and even with vehemence. Moses upbraids the children of Israel because they did not believe the promises of the Lord their God who had brought them up out of the land of Egypt; prophet after prophet complains that the people to whom he was sent would not believe the message of the Lord uttered by his lips; Jesus tells the Jews that if they had believed Moses they would also have believed him; the apostles take up the sad lamentation and bewail the unbelief of those to whom they bore the glad tidings.

The painful fact is patent on every page of human history that the great mass of mankind has never believed what God the Lord has spoken. It is simply impossible for one who by his practical unbelief in what God says makes or treats him as a liar to find eternal blessedness in his presence; for how can two walk together, much less dwell together, except they be agreed? So long as any man lacks confidence in God he will not and cannot desire God's companionship; and companionship with Christ is the blessedness and glory of the Christian's heaven.

It is a common saying that "it makes no difference what a man believes provided his life is right;" but the fact is that men's beliefs control and direct their lives. It is a simple impossibility for a man's life to be right when his beliefs are all wrong. "Truth is in order to godliness," and belief of the truth is the only sure guide into righteousness. Our beliefs exert an absolutely controlling influence upon our lives; they give direction and color to all of our mental activities and moral actions. He who does not believe in the existence of God will never engage in any act of piety or devotion toward a supreme

Being, because the very act of worship involves a mental and moral absurdity. The Thug who believes that murder is right will be sure to act out his belief, and to kill his victim whenever the occasion offers; the Christian who believes it to be his highest duty to obey the commands of God will daily endeavor to live up to his convictions; the man who believes that falsehood is equally as good as the truth will prove to be an habitual liar.

Nothing can be more pernicious than the doctrine that man is not responsible for his belief. If he is not responsible for what he believes, he is not responsible for anything, for without moral opinions he is not a moral agent; and the morality of his actions depends upon his beliefs and desires, from which flows all of his conduct.

The Bible, therefore, is in perfect accord with human experience and history when it presses the paramount importance of faith. While men constantly complain of the justice of God when he asserts that the unbeliever shall be damned, it remains eternally true that if men refuse to believe God their salvation is impossible. The question is frequently and flippantly asked, "Do you believe that God will damn me in hell for ever because I do not believe in Jesus Christ?" God has said, "He that believeth not shall be damned;" and it is far wiser and safer to believe that what God says is true than to believe that he is guilty of falsehood. So far as I can see, the damnation of the unbeliever is simply inevitable. It is no arbitrary caprice on the part of God that makes faith in his Son Jesus Christ a condition of eternal life: "He that hath the Son hath life, and he that hath not the Son of God hath not life." It is well for men to understand that they cannot with safety to their own souls trifle with eternal truth. Whatever else God may be, he must be true. If God should but once fail to be true to his word, and thus deceive us, our confidence in him would be gone, and gone for ever. How dark and dreary and desperate the condition of that man who has lost confidence in God! For him there is nothing but the blackness of darkness. Far less pitiable is the fate of the mariner adrift on mid-ocean without chart or compass or rudder.

The attitude of the soul toward God is decisive of its eternal destiny, and no feature of the life beyond the grave is more strongly marked than the implicit confidence reposed in God by all holy angels and saints and the scornful unbelief of all demons and lost spirits. Heaven is characterized by faith; hell, by distrust of God. Companionship with Christ and all holy beings is the blessedness and the joy of heaven, and without confidence in Christ companionship with him must remain an eternal impossibility. He that believeth not must be damned; to this result the whole moral being of God is irrevocably pledged.

Does any man ask, "Is it possible that so

slight a circumstance as the presence or the absence of faith should make such worldwide and eternal differences in human destiny?" Let him look around and ask what makes such infinite differences in conduct and character here on earth; and if candid, he will confess that they are due to the beliefs of men. The last stage of moral degradation is reached when men believe that darkness is light, that evil is good, that the devil is God; and this belief, wherever it prevails, creates a hell on earth. Let no man be deceived: "God is not mocked; whatsoever a man soweth that shall he also reap." Alienation from God, distrust of him and unbelief in his word will inevitably bring forth a harvest of hopeless misery. The damnation of unbelief is no less certain than the hopelessness of godlessness. Men without God are also without hope, and men without faith are also without life and blessedness. If the picture is dark and dreadful, unbelief in God made it so. No being in this universe with confidence in God is or can be wretched: "He that believeth hath eternal life."

In this age of prevalent and growing unbelief in the threatenings and the promises of God the importance of implicit confidence in his word cannot be too urgently insisted upon or emphasized. Without confidence in God it is impossible to please him.

Few persons can be found who will affirm that these truths are not taught in the word of God, but the moment the duty of believing is pressed upon them they take refuge in the plea that they do not and cannot understand what is meant by confidence in Christ, by faith in God. They do understand what is meant by confidence in a fellow-man, but they cannot comprehend what is meant by confidence in Christ. They imagine that some new faculty is required for the exercise of saving faith in the Lord Jesus Christ, and that without this faculty they cannot believe.

SECTION II.

WHAT, THEN, IS CONFIDENCE IN CHRIST, OR SAVING FAITH?

ONE of the clearest definitions of faith is that given by the Rev. Dr. F. L. Patton in a paper read by him at the First Presbyterian Council at Edinburgh: "Faith is persuasion of the truth. When it terminates on propositions, we call it assent; when on persons, trust." Dr. Archibald Alexander says, "Faith is a belief of the truth." Dr. Dwight calls it "an act of trust or confidence."

It will aid us in this inquiry to recognize and insist upon the fact that every act or exercise of faith is essentially the same in nature. The differences in acts of faith are not in the acts themselves, but in the subject-matter of the truths presented as objects of faith. Confidence in God, considered as an exercise of the soul, differs in no essential element from confidence in a fellow-man: the difference is not in the exercise or the act of faith, but in the object of the faith. In the one case it is God; in the other, it is man. The belief that fire will burn, considered as a subjective exercise of the soul, is in no wise different from the belief that Jesus is the Christ, the Son of the living God. In either case a man is persuaded of the truth on its own proper evidence. In the one case the evidence is derived from personal experience; in the other, from testimony. There is not one set of faculties whereby men are persuaded of natural truths, and another and a different set of faculties whereby they are persuaded of supernatural or divine truths; it is the same faculty that lays hold of every truth, that puts forth every act of confidence. Man in his personality is a unit, and for all purposes this personality is perfect. It is not a part of him, but the whole man, that believes, in every act of faith; it is not one faculty that exercises confidence in man, and a different faculty that exercises confidence in God: in both cases it is the man who believes, confides, trusts.

Of all human acts, faith is one of the simplest and the most common, nor in its everyday use do men find any difficulty in comprehending it. Human life and all of man's activities, occupations and relationships are founded upon and rest securely on faith. Impelled by hunger, men partake of the food which God has provided, believing that it will sustain and nourish life; they are persuaded of this truth, and they act upon this belief. The husbandman believes in the uniformity of nature—that while the earth remaineth seedtime and harvest, cold and heat, summer and winter and day and night shall not cease; and on this belief or confidence he acts: he fallows the ground, sows the seed and gathers the harvest. He is persuaded of a natural truth upon its own appropriate and sufficient evidence, and on this faith he acts in sowing and in reaping. The seamen who do business on the great deep launch forth in the confident belief that water will float the vessel, and that wind and tide and steam will bring them to their desired haven. Here, there is persuasion of the truth, with an act of trust in consequence of the persuasion.

Nearly all business transactions rest upon faith and are conducted upon mutual confidence between man and man. Men deposit money in banks, receive and give notes, drafts and checks, professional men render services, merchants sell their wares, mechanics do work, and all these manifold activities and transactions have their foundation in the confidence reposed by man in his fellow-men. In fact, it is this confidence that holds society together and makes human existence on the earth possible and endurable. Destroy this confidence, and a state far worse than anarchy would at once ensue. No difficulty is experienced as to what is meant in these connections by the words "confidence," "faith," "trust;" the act designated by these is simple and is easily understood.

Yet the moment we speak of confidence, trust in God, men at once declare their inability to comprehend the meaning of this faith. But the faith in its essence as a human act is the same; the personal object is different. In the one case it is our fellow-man; in the other, it is God. If a man is able to know what it is to have confidence in a fellow-mortal, surely he should have no difficulty in knowing what confidence in God means.

Let me use an illustration from every-day life—one employed with signal power by Dr. Mark Hopkins in an article in the *Princeton Review* on "Faith." We are in the habit of saying, "Yes, I know Dr. A.; he is my family physician, in whom I have every confidence. I trust myself and all the members of my family to his care and skill with implicit confidence." Let us analyze this case, for in it we have a most excellent illustration of saving faith in the Lord Jesus Christ as the great Physician of souls.

Dr. A. presents himself to the public as a physician to minister to the ills and the sicknesses of his fellow-mortals. This is his profession, his avocation, his business, and in this character he is known to the public. In some way, either by general reputation or by the testimony of friends or by personal observation, I have acquired knowledge of him, and am persuaded that he is wise, skillful and reliable, and so I trust myself and my family to his care. I have confidence in him in the character in which he presents himself to me. Here there is nothing strange, mysterious or incomprehensible; a child can understand what I mean by confidence in my physician.

So in the case of Jesus Christ of Nazareth, the great Physician. In some way—either by general reputation or by the testimony of friends who have tried him or by the scriptures of the Old and New Testaments—I have obtained knowledge of him as a wise, kind and skillful Physician. True, he is in heaven and I cannot see him with my mortal eyes, but he is a living Person, and he presents himself to me as a Healer and a Saviour. Faith is personal confidence in him in the character in which he is presented to me in the Scriptures. The moment I trust myself to him I have exercised saving faith. If I am persuaded of the truth of the historic propositions concerning him, I have faith, in the sense of "assent" to the propositions; if I confide in him as a personal Saviour, then I have saving faith. "Assent" to truths concerning him is different from the committal of one's self to him. Trust in him is different from belief of statements concerning him: "With the heart man believeth unto righteousness, and with the mouth confession is made unto salvation." All beliefs about Christ come short of salvation until the man commits himself with confiding trust to him. Many persons seem to exercise faith in Christ as regards others, but do not exercise it as regards themselves: they believe that he saves others, but do not believe that he is their Saviour; they believe what is said about him in the sacred Scriptures, but they do not commit themselves to him.

They believe that Dr. A. is a good physician, but have never placed themselves under his care. How many, alas! never place themselves in the hands and under the care of the great Physician Christ Jesus!

Faith is impossible without knowledge: "How shall they believe in him of whom they have not heard? So then faith cometh by hearing, and hearing by the word of God." There can be no "assent" to any proposition unless and until it has been presented to, and apprehended by, the mind; there can be no trust in a person until something is known of that person and of the character in which he is presented to us for our confidence. Any truth presented to man as a proper object of faith must be supported by its own appropriate and sufficient evidence.

SECTION III.

FAITH FOUNDED ON EVIDENCE.

OF course the word "testimony" is not used here in the narrow sense in which it is employed to designate evidence in court, nor even in the wider, but still limited, sense in which it denotes some declaration of our fellow-men, but in the general sense of evidence. Every truth and all truth has its own proper and sufficient evidence, and without evidence men cannot believe. Whatever presents itself to me for my belief must commend itself by appropriate evidence.

In every sphere or realm of knowledge the truths which are the proper objects of belief are authenticated to us by appropriate testimony. In the sphere of the senses truths belonging to this region are authenticated to men by the testimony of the organs of sensation. You believe that a rose is fragrant, that ice is cold, that iron is hard, that matter is divisible, that fire will burn, that honey is sweet, and you believe these truths upon the testimony of your bodily organs, the senses. Through these organs of sensation, either mediately or immediately, you have knowledge of an external world and of its various properties. This knowledge is presented to and established by the testimony of the organs of taste, touch, smell, hearing and sight. Man never asks, nor does he need, any other evidence than that given by his senses to persuade him of the truths that belong to this realm or department of knowledge.

When I pass beyond the bounds of my own personal observation, I am dependent for knowledge upon the testimony of my fellow-men. There are thousands and tens of thousands of truths and facts of which I have no personal knowledge, and yet I receive them upon the testimony of others. I have never seen London Bridge, nor St. Peter's at Rome, nor the Pyramid of Gizeh, nor the Táj Mahál, nor Mount Everest, and yet I am fully persuaded that these objects exist; and this belief is founded upon human testimony. I have never seen Lake Tanganyika, nor the Dead Sea, nor the river Livingstone, and yet I am as certain of their existence as if I had sailed over or bathed in them; and this assurance is based upon the words of others.

So of all that vast domain of knowledge embraced in the history of the past: we are wholly dependent upon the evidence left on record by our fellow-men. No living man, by leagues of space and centuries of time, ever saw or heard Moses, or David, or Nebuchadnezzar, or Cyrus, or Alexander, or Cæsar, or Constantine, or Luther, or Wyckliffe, or Shakespeare, or Bunyan, and yet we believe that Moses was Israel's leader and that David was Jesse's son and king at Hebron, that Nebuchadnezzar built great Babylon, that

Cyrus was a noble emperor, that Alexander conquered the larger portion of the known world, that Cæsar crossed the Rubicon, that Constantine professed and established the Christian religion in the Roman empire, that Luther was the great Reformer, that Wyckliffe gave the first complete English Bible to the England of his day, that Shakespeare wrote *Macbeth* and that John Bunyan gave to the world the *Pilgrim's Progress*. Of these, and of all the facts of the past, we have no personal knowledge, no observation, no experience, but must rely absolutely upon the testimony of others. Yet what man of even a minimum amount of sense fails to receive and to rest with confidence upon these truths authenticated to him by appropriate and sufficient evidence? In this great department of knowledge faith cometh by hearing and hearing by the word of men, and on their testimony we rest with assured confidence. We assent to the propositions presented upon sufficient evidence for our belief.

But there is another department of knowledge—a sphere or realm above that of the organs of sensation, beyond that of human experience: there is a world of which our senses can give no information, concerning which our fellow-men can bear no testimony, because unto this realm the senses do not reach, into this our fellow-mortals cannot enter; or if they enter, they cannot return to bear witness. I allude to that immense sphere or realm above nature to which we give the name of supernatural. What do we know or believe concerning that world which is not bounded by earthly times and earthly spaces? How can we know anything of that realm which lies beyond personal sensation or human observation and testimony?

The would-be wise man who now assumes the name of agnostic, and who modestly and meekly limits human knowledge to what he knows, says at once, "I do not, and I cannot, know anything whatever of the supernatural —of any realm beyond the range of my senses, or perhaps the senses of others: my beliefs and knowledge are limited entirely to the present sphere of nature." The Christian thanks God that there are faith in and knowledge of worlds and beings above and beyond the limitations of earth and time and sense, and this faith is founded upon the testimony of that God who will not, and who cannot, deceive his creatures. If we believe the testimony of men as to natural things, ought we not to believe the testimony of God as to supernatural things? If we believe the testimony of Livingstone and Stanley concerning the lakes, rivers, products and people of Africa, shall we not also receive the testimony of God the Father, Son and Holy Spirit concerning the river and the tree of life in the paradise regained, and concerning the ranks and orders of the holy beings who people the heavenly realms? Shall I believe Stanley when he tells me of the bloody and brutal savages of Uregga and Manyema, and refuse to believe God when he tells me of the demons in hell or the angels and saints in heaven?

I am called upon by every principle of the critical and scientific method to accept the testimony of competent and credible human witnesses concerning all things belonging to the entire sphere of human observation; so also I am called upon by the very same principles to accept the testimony of competent and credible supernatural and divine witnesses concerning things that pertain to the supernatural sphere. If I am bound to believe the testimony of travelers concerning other lands and peoples that I never saw, I am also bound to believe angels, Jesus and the Holy Spirit when they testify as to other worlds and intelligences. And the highest and wisest and most ennobling of all man's beliefs is his faith in the testimony of God. If we receive the witness of men, the witness of God is greater. If there is a God worthy of man's worship, then he must possess in an infinite number and degree all possible perfections, and among them knowledge and truthfulness, and hence he must of necessity be the most competent and credible of all witnesses, human or divine. Therefore, to accept the testimony of God is to have the highest of all possible evidence; not to believe what God says is no less a folly than a sin. This faith is the substance of things hoped for, the evidence of things not seen.

Faith in its largest Bible use is the cordial reception by man of every word spoken by God in the scriptures of the Old and the New Testament: "By faith a Christian believeth to be true whatsoever is revealed in the word, upon the authority of God himself speaking therein." Whether the Bible contains the record of what God has spoken does not belong to this present discussion. To believe what God says of his Son Christ Jesus and to trust Jesus the Lord as a personal Saviour is to possess and exercise saving faith. Confidence in a person differs from assent to a proposition.

Some men believe a part, but not the whole, of God's testimony as contained in his word; they believe certain portions of what he has revealed, and other portions they reject; they accept some of his statements, but reject others; they receive some of the truths taught by Jesus Christ, but refuse to receive others. One may believe that "the worlds were framed by the word of God," and at the same time he may deny that the finally impenitent will be banished from the presence of God; one may believe that Jesus is the Christ, the Son of God, and at the same time deny that "he that believeth not shall be damned;" one may believe what is said of our Lord in the Scriptures, and yet not confide in him for personal salvation.

The Bible everywhere enjoins belief in God's testimony and confidence in his Son our Saviour as the immediate and urgent duty of every human being, and it declares with equal emphasis that unbelief in Christ is a heinous sin. It teaches that unbelief in God is not a guiltless infirmity, but a damnable offence. For unbelief by its acts says to God, "I do not believe what you say, and I will not trust your Son." This is deep and desperate iniquity: it treats God as a liar, it destroys all confidence between man and his Maker, it is the prelude and the preparation for hell: "He that believeth not shall be damned." Of all the fearful sights in this ruined world, none thrills the soul with more unutterable horror than to see a mortal man stand in the presence of his Maker and hear him say to God, "I do not believe what you say, and I will not trust in your Son."

Dr. Mark Hopkins says, "Faith is confidence in a personal being." Now, if we say to a fellow-man—a personal being—"I have no confidence in you," we grossly insult him and render impossible all kindly and friendly intercourse with him. But God is also a "personal being;" and if men show by words or actions that they have no confidence in him, they thereby grievously dishonor him and render companionship and loving communion with him impossible. Unbelief in Jesus Christ—God manifest in the flesh—is the most aggravated form of dishonor done to God as a personal being, and continued unbelief must of necessity for ever exclude the sinner from the blessed and loving presence of God. He that believeth not, not only shall be, but ought to be, damned; and on this ground the condemnation of the wicked is no arbitrary and capricious decree of God, but a natural and inevitable necessity. Any sin, however heinous, may be pardoned through the blood and righteousness of the Son of God, but even in the infinite grace of God there is no provision made to save the willful and persistent unbeliever in the Lord Jesus Christ. If men do not have confidence in Christ, how is it possible for him to be their Saviour? "If any man love not the Lord Jesus Christ, let him be Anathema. Maran atha."

SECTION IV.

THREE VIEWS OF FAITH—THE ROMISH, THE RATIONALISTIC, THE CHRISTIAN.

THE *Romish view* is that God has appointed the Church of Rome his infallible visible representative among men, and that all men everywhere are bound to believe what the Church teaches upon her authority as an infallible teacher. According to this theory, the dogma of Church authority is the foundation of faith: men must believe what the Church teaches, and simply because the Church teaches it. Beyond and above the authority of the Church there is no tribunal to which the soul can appeal. The Church affirms: I must believe; the Church commands: I must obey. The teachings of the Church of Rome may flatly contradict the testimony of my senses, may contradict the judgment of my reason, may contradict all my conclusions concerning truths of every kind, but I must renounce all these testimonies and conclusions at the command of this Church, and accept her dogmas as ultimate infallible truth simply and solely upon her decree.

The authority of the Church is to dominate the senses, intellect, conscience and will of men. After the priest has pronounced the words of consecration and changed the little piece of bread—the wafer—into the "body and Godhead of Christ," it is in vain that my senses as before testify that the bread is still bread, that the wafer looks like bread, smells like bread, tastes like bread, and all this in that sphere or realm where only the senses have a right to be heard : Rome stands with her dogmas of authority, and says, "This wafer is no longer bread : it has been changed into the body, blood and divinity of our Lord, into a *totum Christum*—a whole Christ:

you must reject the testimony of your senses and believe what the Church says."

Thousands of intelligent Romanists who are entitled to credence profess to believe this upon the authority of the Church, and it is at least a most interesting mental problem whether they really do believe this dogma of the Church or the testimony of their senses. Can they possibly believe that to be a God which their senses declare to be only bread? Is it possible for man to believe that to be true which thus so directly contradicts the evidence of his senses—the very organs, and the only organs, whereby he can obtain any knowledge whatever of the properties of bread? Do men acquire knowledge of the properties of bread through the organs of taste, smell, sight and touch, or through the teachings of an infallible Church?

It must be evident to every intelligent and candid person that the mere authority of the so-called Church is no sufficient and firm foundation upon which to erect any structure of faith; yet this is the stone on which in great part is laid the faith of the papal hierarchy and its subjects. From the dogma of Church authority there may grow a gigantic and baleful superstition, but never an intelligent faith; and the blind and unquestioning belief and obedience of the slaves of the papacy are as far removed from intelligent Christian faith as are the blasphemous utterances of the most avowed and arrant infidel. "Faith cometh by hearing, and hearing by the word of God." A system that starts thus with the denial of the truthfulness of the testimony of our senses and reason in their proper sphere is unworthy of the confidence of mankind and deserves the reprobation of the race.

2. *The Rationalistic View.*—Rationalism founds faith entirely on human reason. Its fundamental dogma is, "Not merely that which contradicts human reason, but whatever is above or beyond that reason—whatever is insoluble by reason—is incredible." Chris-

tianity would not dissent if rationalism contented itself with the affirmation that whatever contradicts the testimony of reason is incredible, for it is the perfection of folly to suppose that the reason of man can accept as true that which he knows to be false. If a man said that he believed a circle was square or that an effect had no producing cause, this would be equivalent to saying that his reason accepted as true what his reason knew to be not only absurd, but impossible.

But the objection is at hand, "Does not this admission with one fell stroke destroy all faith in the vital doctrines of the Christian religion?" Are not many of the truths of the Bible contradictory of human reason? And does not infidelity declare against these doctrines because of their conflict with reason? The mode of the divine existence—three subsistencies in one essence—the incarnation of the Son of God, the coexistence of divine efficiency and human freedom, the immutability of God and the efficacy of prayer,—are not these and their correlated truths in direct conflict with and in contradiction of human reason? At this point let the distinction between that which *contradicts* reason and that which is *above* reason be clearly and carefully noted : a truth may be *above* reason, and yet not *contradict* reason. I may be unable to explain the mode of the divine existence, and yet when it is revealed to me as a fact upon competent and credible evidence there is nothing that *contradicts* the testimony of my reason, though there is much that is above and beyond my highest powers of reason. So I may be unable to originate the idea of the Word made flesh ; but when that life is manifested and men see and hear and handle the incarnate Son of God, I can accept their testimony and believe that Jesus of Nazareth is the Christ, the Son of God. I may be unable to solve the problem of the coexistence of divine purpose and efficiency with human freedom and responsibility ; but when both truths are established upon separate and sufficient evidence, my reason is bound to accept them. In these cases there is something above, but nothing contradictory of, my reason. It by no means follows that what is insoluble by reason is in conflict with and contradiction of human reason: insolubility and contradiction are not synonymous terms. Every man believes upon sufficient evidence many things that he cannot comprehend.

Now, rationalism denies the reality of knowledge or faith outside the limited sphere of nature, reason and human experience. Not content with affirming as regards this sphere that whatever contradicts reason is incredible, it also denies the possibility of certain knowledge of anything outside this realm. In short, it denies the possibility of God and a supranatural world.

The real point at issue is not whether it is possible to believe that which contradicts reason, but whether reason can and ought to accept truths above and beyond itself upon the testimony of supranatural beings. The existence of God, of angels and of demons, the Godhead of Jesus, the judgment of the last day, heaven and hell, are facts that lie beyond the finite realm—the realm of nature, time and sense—but we accept them as facts upon adequate evidence; nor do they contradict anything that we know or believe upon the testimony of our senses or reason.

3. The *Christian* and *common-sense* view proceeds upon the fundamental fact that all rational faith must rest upon sufficient evidence, that man believes nothing, and can believe nothing, that is not authenticated to him by its own appropriate and sufficient evidence. Whoever accepts a fact in the sphere of the senses believes upon the testimony of his organs of sensation. If the fact is in the realm of consciousness, the man believes upon the testimony of his consciousness; if the fact is in the domain of history, he believes upon the testimony of competent and credible witnesses; if the fact is in the

sphere of the supranatural, then he believes upon the testimony of supranatural beings. This view subjects the faith of the Christian to every ascertained and accepted law of scientific knowledge and rational belief. It does not ask from its adherents irrational superstition or blind credulity; it demands from no one faith in that which contradicts all or any of the established laws of human thought. It always presents evidence before it requires faith, and is ready to give to every man a reason for what it believes. Without knowledge and evidence there cannot be faith.

According to this view, in the sphere of the senses man believes upon the evidence of sensation; in the sphere of consciousness, upon the evidence of consciousness; in the sphere of the human, upon the evidence of his fellow-mortal; in the sphere of the divine, upon the testimony of God.

Christianity rejects with abhorrence the dogma of ecclesiastical authority, and denies that man can and must believe the unbelievable upon the decree of any pope, council, synod or assembly. It holds fast to the word of the Lord that faith cometh by hearing—by hearing appropriate, competent and credible testimony; that it comes in this way, and cannot possibly come in any other way. It rejects the doctrine that all faith is founded solely in and on human reason; it rejects the assertion that knowledge and belief are limited to the things of earth and sense, and that man's mind cannot believe anything that his mind cannot fully comprehend and solve; it affirms potency outside of man and matter; and believes in the reality of knowledge and faith respecting objects in the realm above and beyond the finite.

SECTION V.

THE TESTIMONY OF GOD.

WE are thus brought face to face with the questions, "Has God ever spoken to man? Has he ever in words revealed himself and his will to mortals? Is there anywhere on earth in the possession of men any testimony of God?" It does not fall within the scope of this work to discuss these questions; suffice it to say that the great majority of those who have investigated the subject of the genuineness and authenticity of the books of the sacred Scriptures express themselves as abundantly satisfied on these points. If men receive human testimony as to the authenticity of any books, then it is confidently asserted that the evidence in favor of the books of the Bible is far more abundant both in kind and in degree than that in behalf of any other books on earth; if any works among men can be authentic, these must be.

Whatever these books may or may not be, they do at least contain a large and most important mass of human testimony on subjects of the most vital interest to man? If these books are genuine and authentic—as nearly all educated and candid men admit—then we are called to consider the testimony handed down to us by Moses, Samuel, David, Isaiah, Daniel, Matthew, Luke, John and Paul concerning what God said and did. If the things alleged to have occurred did actually transpire in the past, then the only possible method by which we of the present can have knowledge of them is upon the testimony of men who lived in the past, and who were competent and credible witnesses.

The simple issue here is this: "Can we believe the statements made by these men? Can we accept their testimony concerning what God said and did? Can we believe them when they tell us of what they saw and heard and handled of the Word of life?" These men present themselves to us in the attitude of competent and credible witnesses; and if we accept their testimony and believe their statements, then we are transported back to the ages in which they lived, and see with their eyes, hear with their ears and handle with their hands. With them we are face to face with God, and see his works and hear his words and handle his form.

I will not insult the intelligence of the weakest-minded of mortals by hinting that if the God who made him should draw near in human form and speak in audible voice to him time and again it would be impossible for him to know that God, and so I will not insult the intelligence of my readers by proving that Moses could know God when he spoke face to face with him, or that Peter, James and John could know God when they saw him, or that Thomas and other disciples could know God when they handled him. If man can know anything, he can surely know the Father God in whose image he was made; and if God can do anything, surely he can make himself known to his child. If this be not true, then all knowledge is impossible and life is a delusion and a lie.

Assuming, then, the reliability of these sacred records and the truthfulness of these witnesses, we have in our hands the testimony of God himself—what he said and what he did—and the important practical questions are, "Do we believe what God says in his word to men? Do we believe God to be just what his words and works declare him to be? Do we confide in him as thus he reveals himself to us?" If we thus believe and confide, we have faith.

The phrase "I believe the Bible" admits of two very different constructions. By these words, one man may mean that he accepts as authentic the Bible records and receives as true the testimony of the writers, but he does not intend to say that he believes all that God affirms in the word. There are multitudes who receive the Bible as true without believing all that God says; they accept the human, but not the divine, testimony contained in the Scriptures.

By the phrase "I believe the Bible" another man means that he accepts as true what the human witnesses testify, and he also receives and believes all that God says; he accepts both the human and the divine testimony. A man may believe what the witnesses and writers say, and yet he may not believe what God said to them. Thousands of the children of Israel believed that God spoke to Moses and others of their prophets; they believed that these prophets reported to them the very words of God, and at the same time they did not believe the message of the Lord as delivered to them by the prophets. The illustrations of this fact are so numerous and familiar that they need not be cited. Even now, there are men who have no doubt that God teaches in his word certain doctrinal truths, but they dislike these truths and do not hesitate to say that they do not believe them, thus refusing to receive the testimony of God himself.

One of my fellow-men may repeat to me something that a neighbor has said about me; I may believe that the neighbor did say what he is reported to have said, and at the same time not believe what the neighbor said. Now, if we accept as true the testimony of the sacred writers, we are face to face, as they were, with God, and the simple point to be pressed in this connection is, "Can, and do, we believe what God says?" It is perfectly manifest that faith may be more or less complete; it may believe all or only part of what God says. There are very few persons, if any, who at all times in their lives believe all that God says.

As was said, a man may believe part of God's testimony, but not all of it. He may believe that God does possess some of the attributes that he claims, but that he does not possess others equally as important; he may believe fully in the love of God, but not in his retributive justice; he may accept the doctrine of the believer's salvation, and at the same time reject the statement of the unbeliever's damnation; he may receive much of what God reveals concerning himself, and at the same time have no personal confidence in him.

Faith is perfect when it believes all that God says and trusts fully in him, and no man has Christian faith until he has personal confidence in Christ. The testimony of God centres and is summed up in Christ: he is the Revealer of God, the way, the truth, and the life; and no man cometh unto the Father but by him. In short, he is God manifest in the flesh, and he that sees and knows him sees and knows the Father also. The gracious purpose of God in all his wondrous testimony recorded in the Scriptures is to lead men to accept, to trust, to have confidence in, Christ: "This was written that ye might believe that Jesus is the Christ, the Son of God," and that ye might have confidence that Christ is all that he claims to be, and that he will do all he promises to do; and unless a man has this he is guilty of the sin of unbelief.

A man desiring to sail for Europe might stand upon the pier in New York, and, looking at one of the magnificent ocean-steamers lying in port, would have confidence in her seaworthiness, speed and comfort; he might also have confidence in the skill and fidelity of the captain; but all this would fail to land him in Liverpool: he could not cross the ocean until by an act of the will he put himself aboard the vessel and confided himself to the care of the captain. So the sinner who desires to reach the heavenly port must by an act of his own, exercise confidence in the great Captain of our salvation and trust him for all that is needed to bring him to his desired haven. Any faith short of this commitment of one's self to the Lord Jesus does not save the sinner.

To believe something else about Christ, or to believe something else that Christ has said or something else that Christ has promised to do for some other person, cannot possibly take the place of your personal trust and commitment of yourself to him: "With the heart man believeth unto righteousness, and with the mouth confession is made unto salvation."

Dr. Mark Hopkins, in the September number of the *Princeton Review* for 1878, in one of the ablest articles ever written on the subject of faith, says:

"Of course the confidence or trust of one personal being in another may be of every degree, according to the ground of it in the person trusted and to the relations in which they are placed. Suppose, then, the relation to be that of physician and patient, with entire confidence on the part of the patient. He will then believe what the physician may say, will take any remedy he may prescribe and will do whatever he directs.

"Take, again, the case of a traveler and a guide. If the traveler accepts the guide in full confidence, the forest may be dense and pathless, he may be turned round so that the south shall seem to be north and the east west; yet he will move on without faltering. So, too, with the man who lends money or deposits treasure on the simple word of another, or perhaps even without a word.

"In each of these instances it will be seen that there was a joint-action of the intellect and the will: of the intellect, in a belief involving some interest requiring action; and of the will, in choice and volition with reference to that action. Is, then, the essential element of the faith to be found in the action of the intellect or of the will? Of the will, certainly—so far, at least, that the action of the will cannot be dispensed with and faith remain. True, mere belief is sometimes in the Bible called faith, but it is *dead faith*.

Even the devils have faith in the sense of mere belief.

"The faith of the Scriptures calls for and requires acceptance, commitment and obedience, for God does not reveal anything for the mere purpose of being believed.

"To be the faith of the Bible, belief, whatever its origin, must pass on and up into a loving obedience to God, so drawing in the whole man.

"Confidence in Christ is faith, and this reveals itself in belief of his word, in the commitment of ourselves to him and in obedience to his commands."

SECTION VI.

FAITH NOT A MERE ACT, BUT A LIFE.

IT is a great mistake to suppose, as many do, that faith is a mere act, and that it ends once for all with the committal of the soul to Christ. The sinner who has once trusted Christ will continue to trust him—having once confided in him, will continue to confide in him. The confidence of the sinner in his Saviour ever grows and increases in strength and sweetness. This confidence, once begotten in the soul by the Holy Spirit, abides eternally.

"The clouds may come and go,
   And storms may sweep the sky;
The blood-sealed friendship changes not:
   The cross is ever nigh."

The believer finds the Saviour more and more worthy of his confidence as the years go by. Other friends in whom we trust may fail and disappoint and deceive us, but the Christ will not, and cannot: he is the same yesterday, to-day and for ever. Through time and eternity he will never do anything to weaken or to destroy that faith which he has originated in the human soul; he is not only the Author, but also the Finisher, of our Faith.

There has been much idle and valueless controversy over the questions, "Does faith precede repentance, or repentance faith? or do both precede or follow regeneration, or, as it is sometimes called, conversion or change of heart?"

It would seem to be undeniable that life must precede action, and spiritual life must exist prior to spiritual activities; the sinner must have spiritual life before he can perform spiritual acts. In the order of thought, then, the new birth and life must go before the forthputting of any spiritual actions, and, since faith and repentance are both spiritual acts, they must follow regeneration. But as a matter of fact, and not of thought, it seems to be impossible to separate the three—regeneration, faith, repentance; they are simultaneous, synchronous. The moment the sinner is regenerated by the Holy Spirit, that moment he believes, that moment he repents. It is useless, therefore, to waste time in discussing the order of succession of regeneration, faith and repentance, when in all actual Christian experience there is no succession, but simultaneity.

The prophet Habakkuk says the just— i. e. the justified man—shall live by his faith; in other words, his faith is his life. The apostle Paul declares that believers walk by faith, and, giving expression to his own deepest experience in this momentous matter, uses these words in his letter to the Galatian churches: "I am crucified with Christ; nevertheless I live; yet not I, but Christ liveth in me, and the life which I now live in the flesh I live by the faith of the Son of God, who loved me and gave himself for me." These words almost identify his faith and his life, and almost identify his life and the life of the Son of God. These passages certainly prove that faith is not a mere act, but is also a life.

The eleventh chapter of the letter to the Hebrews abounds in striking illustrations of this truth. The believing saints whose names and works are here recorded walked all the days of their earthly pilgrimage in the might and reality of faith; this principle guided their steps and controlled their lives. If the faith could be eliminated from their lives, how little would remain! Through faith they subdued kingdoms, wrought righteousness, obtained promises, stopped the mouths of lions, quenched the power of fire, escaped the edge of the sword, from weakness were made strong, waxed mighty in war, turned to flight armies of aliens, received their dead raised to life again.

The faith of these saints was no one single act far back at the commencement of their spiritual existence, but a constant, continuous committal of themselves to God and of obedience to his commands. From the day that God called Abram out of Ur of the Chaldees until the day that the patriarch was laid to rest in the cave of Machpelah his faith was his very life. So powerful and pervading was this principle of faith that it was to these saints throughout their entire earthly pilgrimage, the *substance* of the things they hoped for, the *evidence* of things they had never seen. Faith so guided, colored and controlled their hearts and actions that it was their very life: the just lives by his faith.

Is it not true that every man is what he believes—not merely that his beliefs regulate his conduct, but that they so regulate and control it as to be his life? Our beliefs give motives to all our actions and direct and mould our lives: "As a man thinketh in his heart, so is he."

It is quite popular in these days to speak in terms half of pity and half of contempt of the old-fashioned folks who attach importance to an orthodox faith. All such persons are sadly behind the times now that infidelity, under the specious names of "progress" and "free thought," derides all forms of well-established belief as relics of barbarism and superstition. In high places and low, out of the pulpit, and sometimes in it, it is held as conclusive evidence of cleverness and culture to ridicule the wisdom of the past and to sneer at any man who believes the well-attested and authenticated dogmas of divine truth. Public sentiment exclaims, "It makes no difference what a man's faith is, so that his life is right; it matters not what he believes, provided he does what is right." As if it were possible to separate faith and conduct, beliefs and acts, principles and practices! All human history proves the impossibility of making this separation: you cannot divorce a man's conduct from his

FAITH NOT A MERE ACT. 61

beliefs. His life is the natural outcome of his creed.

No matter how good and how upright a man's general conduct might be, you would not employ him as the confidential clerk of an immense business if you knew that it was one of his unalterably settled beliefs that it was eminently proper and right for a confidential clerk to make free, for his personal use, with the funds of the firm employing him. The most liberal free-thinker who scoffs at everything like a right faith would hesitate—for a while, at least—before he employed this man as chief clerk. Nay, the conviction might possibly get into his head —so full of "free thought"—that in this one particular case it did make some difference what his clerk believed. What general of an army would send on duty to a most important position a subaltern who should gravely inform him that it was one of his fundamental and fixed beliefs that it was eminently right and proper for a soldier to desert his post when he was in danger and felt like leaving? Few juries or judges would attach weight to the testimony of a witness who just as he took the oath told them that he had no conscientious scruples against perjury and did not believe that it was criminal to lie. No sensible man would select as his partner for life the loveliest of womankind who held the doctrines of free love, and who did not believe in the binding obligation of the seventh commandment. What a man believes makes the widest possible difference in human conduct, life and destiny. If belief is wrong, conduct cannot be right. As a man believeth in his heart, so is he; for in the long run he lives out his beliefs.

The devil is now very busy proclaiming and propagating the doctrine, "If a man is sincere, it makes no difference what religion he professes." According to the "father of lies," sincerity, and not truth, is the final and infallible test of religion. Not the man who has clean hands and a pure heart, who works righteousness and obeys God, but the man who is sincere, is acceptable to God and an heir of eternal life. According to this satanic and popular opinion, if the sincerity of a man be sufficiently deep and genuine, then vice is virtue, darkness is light, error is truth, hell is heaven and the devil is God. The most revolting crimes that ever cursed our earth were committed by men deeply in earnest and thoroughly sincere. The cruelties of the Inquisition, the atrocities of Alva in the Netherlands, the Massacre of St. Bartholomew, the assassination of William the Silent, the judicial murder of Jesus the Christ, the ferocious wars of Islam, the human sacrifices of the Druids, the bloody rites of the savages of Africa, the cannibalism of the Pacific islanders, can all be vindicated, justified and approved if the sincerity of the actors constitutes the righteousness of their actions.

It is more than doubtful if the sincerest of all believers in the "sincerity" doctrine would say to the "sincere" and conscientious thief who was making off with his watch, pocket-book and plate, "Friend, go in peace. You are sincere in your belief that it is right for you to steal, and I have no business to interfere with your conscientious convictions." He who believes that the sincerity of a wretch is the only test of truth and righteousness is not far from the road that leads down to the lowest depth of mental and moral degradation possible to man in this mortal state of existence. Beyond any question, men act on and act out their beliefs: according to these, so are their lives; hence it is that the word of God insists with so much emphasis and earnestness on right beliefs and righteous principles, even declaring that without faith it is impossible to please God. Now, the faith of the Christian, so far from being a mere transient act, becomes a fixed and abiding principle of his mental and moral constitution; it is a life—a continuous life—outlasting earth and time and sense.

We sometimes hear the expression concerning the future life that "faith will be lost in fruition," and this is true, if limited in its application to those things promised the child of God as parts of his heritage in the heavenly realm. When he shall have obtained and entered into the possession and enjoyment of what has been promised him, and for which, in confident faith, he now hopes, then faith as to these objects will cease. But faith as a life of confidence in God will never end; throughout eternity the finite will exercise faith in the Infinite, man will believe his Maker and God, the sinner saved by grace will confide in the wisdom and love of his Saviour.

The principle that binds all holy intelligences in one brotherhood of loving allegiance to God is their profound and implicit confidence in him. "Just as gravitation is to the material creation its conserving power and central force, so this faith is the preserving bond of the spiritual universe." If this confidence in God should be destroyed or cease, there would immediately ensue a confusion and an anarchy far more dreadful and destructive than those which would follow the loss of the law of gravitation from its place in the physical creation; the spiritual universe would be in ruins, and would remain in ruins until confidence were restored.

It is true that in the exercise of almighty power God could preserve his throne, but his empire would be one of force, not of loving confidence and communion; and what God wishes in his kingdom is not the fear and submission of slaves, but the affection and confidence of sons. The time will never come when the child's faith in his heavenly Father will cease.

SECTION VII.

FAITH THE DIFFERENTIA OF CHRISTIAN LIFE.

IF called on to point out the distinguishing element of that life which is called "Christian," we should answer without hesitation, "*Faith*." This differentiates the Christian life from all other kinds of life; this is the specific element without which no one is or can be a Christian: "He that believeth hath eternal life, and he that believeth not is condemned already." Jesus said to the unbelieving Jews, "Ye believe not, because ye are not of my sheep."

We are profoundly ignorant of the essence of that strange and wonderful phenomenon to which we give the name of "life." We cannot grasp and hold and analyze it, and yet we can see, examine and understand its manifestations; and, since these manifestations are different in the various forms of living things and persons, we say there are different kinds of life. There is some element in the life of every living thing that differentiates the form or kind to which it appertains from all other forms or kinds of life. When we speak of the *nature* of any particular species of living things or beings, we always have reference to this differentiating element, though we may be unable to define it. The nature of the life of a flower differs from that of an animal; the nature of mere animal life differs from that of man; the nature of human life differs from that of Christian life; and that element which distinguishes and differentiates Christian life from all other forms of life on earth is confidence in Christ.

In all plants there is a vital principle to which we give the name of "vegetable life," and in all the individuals of this group there is sameness of qualities. We give different names to the various members of this species —corn, wheat, rye, barley, sunflower, rose, geranium, etc.—but no individual is entitled to a place in the group unless it is possessed of vegetable life, and that life manifested in certain unvarying forms. In this group there may be, and there are, widely-differing forms, but there is identity or sameness of life, and the element common to all the individuals of the group is the differentia of the species.

Just above the vegetable is the animal species, or that group of living beings possessed of certain common qualities, all animals having an essential identity or sameness of qualities proceeding from their nature. Here, again, differences are observed, but there is identity of qualities. And there is some element here that distinguishes the animal from the vegetable. There is a fundamental difference between the vegetable and the animal, between vegetable life and animal life. Passing to a still higher sphere, we reach rational life. Here the element that differentiates this life is reason, and this life differs in certain qualities from either vegetable life or animal life. So, again, in the still higher realm of spiritual life there is a specific quality that distinguishes this from all other kinds of life, whether vegetable, animal or rational, and this quality is faith. All persons possessed of this vital principle are believers or Christians and have eternal life derived from the heavenly Man Christ Jesus, who is a quickening Spirit. Whoever is destitute of this living principle of faith has no right whatever to the name of "believer;" he who has not the Spirit of Christ is none of his. Whatever is destitute of the principle of vegetable life is not a vegetable; whatever is destitute of the principle of animal life is not an animal; whoever is destitute of the principle of rational life is not a rational being; and whosoever is destitute of the living principle of faith is not a Christian. Here confidence in Christ marks and separates the Christian from all other men, and Christian life from all other kinds of life.

However much Christians may resemble one another or may differ in certain qualities, they all agree, and must agree, in the possession of this common principle of faith to entitle them to a name and a place in that group of individuals to which we give the name of "Christian."

Just as there are various degrees in the strength, health and force of all forms of vegetable, animal and rational life, so here also there are various degrees of power in the life of faith; its manifestations differ most widely in different individuals of the group. As there are great varieties of plants, animals and men, so there are many varieties of Christians: there are babes in Christ, there are carnal Christians, there are weak believers, there are full-grown and mature disciples; but all these, whether with much faith or with little faith, with weak life or with robust life, are Christians. It is not the degree of the confidence reposed in Christ, it is not the strength or the weakness of the faith, but the faith itself, that marks the child of God. We say it is wholly unnatural for a child not to have faith in his father, but it is far more unnatural—yea, it is impossible—for a Christian not to have confidence in his Redeemer.

SECTION VIII.

FAITH'S WARRANT IS GOD'S WORD.

"DOES Christ authorize our confidence?" is a fundamental and most important inquiry. Men sometimes exercise unauthorized confidence in their fellow-men, and are sadly disappointed. A man may believe from what he knows of his friend that he will assist him in a certain business transaction, and on the strength of that belief may go forward, make contracts and incur obligations; but when he calls upon his friend for the expected funds, the friend declines to let him have the money. The gentleman has no just cause of complaint; his friend never authorized him to expect this assistance. It is an all-important question, therefore, to settle: "Has God authorized my confidence?" This question answered, then I wish to know to what extent he warrants this confidence and where I shall find this warrant. Faith must find its warrant in God's word. In his word God reveals himself to man, makes promises and places himself under obligations to him. Man has the right, therefore, to exercise confidence in God to the utmost extent authorized in the sacred Scriptures.

If my fellow-man, in whose ability and good-will I have confidence, gave me his word that he would do certain things for me, I should have the right, and it would be my duty, to exercise full confidence to the very extent of the promises: not to believe his word and confide in him would be to distrust his veracity and to impeach his integrity. But if I made demands upon him without his authorizing these demands, my conduct would be liable to the charge of presumption.

In his word God has authorized the children of men to confide in him and in his Son Jesus Christ. He warrants us, according to our needs, to call upon him, and promises to supply those needs according to his riches in glory by Christ Jesus.

On a remarkable occasion when our Lord's disciples could not cast out a devil he said to them, "If ye have faith as a grain of mustard-seed, ye shall say unto this mountain, Remove hence to yonder place, and it shall remove; and nothing shall be impossible to you." The warrant for faith is undoubtedly a very large one, and the sin that has so easily beset all Christians in all ages has been the sin of unbelief. So far as salvation is concerned, every one is authorized to trust Christ; for his own promise is, "Him that cometh to me I will in no wise cast out." Christians, however, often say, "Oh yes; I believe that God will do this for me;" yet when you ask them why they think thus, they can give no intelligent reason for their belief. They are unable to find anywhere in God's word a warrant for their faith; there is no promise or word of God to authorize such confidence. In such a case the Christian has been, not believing, but presuming upon God. "Cast thyself down from this pinnacle of the temple; you shall not be injured: 'He shall give his angels charge over thee, to keep thee; in their hands they shall bear thee up, lest at any time thou dash thy foot against a stone;'" but the answer is, "It is written, Thou shalt not tempt the Lord thy God."

The general rule, and the safe one, is that all faith must find its warrant in the written word of God. To the utmost extent that confidence is thus authorized it will never be disappointed: "Whosoever believeth on him shall not be ashamed." Christ's command to Peter to come to him on the water was a sufficient warrant to that disciple to walk upon the waves in the fullest confidence that they would bear him up, and so long as his confidence that Christ was mightier than the waves remained unshaken he walked with safety. God had authorized this confidence, but this does not warrant every Christian to walk upon the sea.

SECTION IX.

THE ASSURANCE OF FAITH.

THE assurance of faith is most intimately connected with the warrant of faith. If I believe the word of God, may I not also have certain knowledge that I do believe it? When I confide in my physician, do I know that I have confidence in him? When I confide in Christ as my spiritual Physician, do I know that I thus confide in him? If a person said to you that he believed the sun would rise to-morrow morning, would he not think it a very strange question if you should ask him if he *knew* that he believed this?

There are many who hold the opinion that the knowledge of our beliefs cannot be separated from the beliefs themselves—that every act of belief by man is attended with the knowledge that he does thus believe. Paul's statement on the subject of the assurance of faith is this: "I know whom I have believed, and am persuaded that he is able to keep that which I have committed unto him against that day." The apostle John testifies, "We know that the Son of God is come, and hath given us an understanding that we may know him that is true; and we are in him that is true, even in his Son Jesus Christ." The apostolic Christians were not strangers to the doctrine of the assurance of faith; they not only believed, but they knew that they believed—not only trusted Christ, but knew that they trusted him.

It is needless to multiply quotations from the Scriptures to prove that it is the privilege of the believer to have the assurance of faith, to know that he has believed, to know that he has confided in the Lord Jesus Christ. Why should assured knowledge in the domain of Christian experience be thought a thing impossible?

The consensus of the faith of the Reformed churches is thus scripturally expressed: "Such as truly believe in the Lord Jesus, and love him in sincerity, endeavoring to walk in all good conscience before him, may in this life be certainly assured that they are in a state of grace. . . . This infallible assurance of faith is founded upon the divine truth of the promises of salvation, the inward evidence of those graces unto which these promises are made, the testimony of the Spirit of adoption witnessing with our spirits that we are the children of God."—*Confession of Faith, chap. xviii.*

So far from this being an extreme statement of this doctrine, many of the Reformers held and taught "that to believe is to be assured of our own personal salvation," "that faith and assurance were inseparably connected." This doctrine is taught in the Augsburg Confession and in the Heidelberg Catechism and was held by Luther, Melanchthon and Calvin. The fact will scarcely be questioned by intelligent persons that the times of the greatest spirituality in the life of the Church have been the occasions when this grace of assurance was most generally possessed and most largely enjoyed. When the fires of persecution were kindled upon believers, the question of their personal relation to their Redeemer was to them not a matter of doubt, but of certainty; they were enabled to say, "We know whom we have believed."

Periods of coldness, worldliness and declension in the Church have always been characterized by the absence of this assurance from the conscious experience of Christians. In all earthly matters men have assured knowledge, assured belief, assured hopes; surely they ought to have the same certainty in relation to spiritual and eternal interests. Man ought to be as certain that he believes God, as he is that he believes his fellow-man. The ground of assurance is not in the believer himself, but in the sure promise of that God who cannot possibly prove faithless to his

THE ASSURANCE OF FAITH.

own word. If we believe not, yet he abideth faithful; he cannot deny himself. The certainty of any believer's salvation rests, not upon himself, but absolutely upon the promise of Christ to save him; and if his salvation is perfectly assured in Christ, he can surely be certain that it is thus assured. When the traveler steps on the steamer, he knows that he is on board. When I give my treasures in trust to a friend, I know that I confide them to his custody. When I commit my soul-treasures to Christ, I ought to know that I have trusted them to him.

It is true that many professed Christians are perfect strangers to this grace of assurance, but we must remember that there are many who profess Christ who do not possess him: "Many will say to me in that day, Lord, Lord, have we not prophesied in thy name? and in thy name have cast out devils? and in thy name done many wonderful works? and then will I profess unto them, I never knew you." "Not every one that saith unto me,

Lord, Lord, shall enter into the kingdom of heaven." The fact, therefore, that many mere professors who know not Christ and never confided in him do not have this assurance is no evidence whatever against the truth of the doctrine. Of course it is impossible for them to have the assurance of salvation while they are unsaved; they cannot possibly know that they possess that of which they really are utterly destitute.

Again, there are many true believers in our Lord who live such unspiritual, worldly and inconsistent lives that they fail to realize and to enjoy many of the blessed privileges of redemption, and among them this one of assurance. "If we say that we have fellowship with Him and walk in darkness, we lie, and do not the truth." The Christian who is walking in sin loses fellowship with God, and with that he loses the joy of salvation and the blessedness of assurance. When he is walking in the light, in conscious communion with Christ, and only then, can he be

THE ASSURANCE OF FAITH. 83

assured of his salvation as his present possession.

It is sad to see so many Christians walking all their days in doubt of their acceptance with God through the righteousness of their risen Redeemer. The believer who thus passes his life in doubt and darkness will prove as fruitless a worker in the harvest of the Lord, as the farmer who, doubting his rightful title to his farm, should spend all of his time, not in cultivating the soil, but in searching the recorded deeds to his property. Our Father in heaven desires the joyous service of his loving children who know that they are his children, and who can say from confiding hearts, "Abba, Father."

Nor is there, as some think, the slightest approach to presumption in the exercise of this filial confidence. When the eyes of the blind man were opened and he saw the blessed light of the sun, was it presumption for him to say, "One thing I know, that whereas I was blind, now I see; a man that is called

Jesus said unto me, Go to the pool of Siloam, and wash: and I went and washed, and I received sight"?

When the father said of the younger son who had come home, "This my son was dead and is alive again, he was lost and is found," it was not presumption, but the proper thing for the son to do, to accept the ring and robe and the name and place of a son, and to say that he was a son, not a servant; anything else than this would have been to doubt his father's word and to distrust his forgiving love.

Surely it is the farthest possible from presumption, when Christ says to the pardoned penitent, "Go in peace, thy sins are forgiven thee," for that penitent joyfully to obey the command and to walk in the assured knowledge of pardon, acceptance and sonship. As the child of an earthly father is assured of that father's love, so ought the child of God to be always assured of the love of the heavenly Father; and if he is walking in cheerful obedience to the will of God, he cannot be a stranger to the assurance of his Father's love. The obedient, trustful, loving child is always conscious of the father's love.

It would be an unspeakable blessing to the Church of this day could this precious doctrine of assurance have the same prominence now that it held in the teachings of the Reformers of the sixteenth century, and that it occupies in the inspired word of God.

SECTION X.

THE GROWTH OF FAITH.

WITH the exception of the eternal life of God, so far as we have knowledge, growth is the law of everything that has life. Every living thing not only has the capacity for growth, but it *grows*. The germ, whether of grass, flower, herb, tree, animal or man, does not, if possessed of life, remain a mere germ, but the living power in the germ manifests itself, makes itself known, in the various forms of life—first the blade, then the ear, after that the full corn in the ear. There is growth from the very beginning to the full maturity of life; the universal law is, "Where there is life there must be growth;" and faith as a life in the believer is no exception to this law.

THE GROWTH OF FAITH.

The Christian is a new creature in Christ Jesus; he has a new life from the risen Redeemer, the heavenly Man; hence he is subject to the law of growth, and is exhorted to grow in grace and in the knowledge of our Lord and Saviour Jesus Christ. He must go on to maturity, to the measure of a full-grown man: the babe in Christ must, and will, attain to manhood in him.

The apostle Paul, writing to the Christians at Corinth, says, "And I, brethren, could not speak unto you as unto spiritual, but as unto carnal, even as unto babes in Christ; I have fed you with milk, and not with meat." The words "spiritual" and "carnal" are here used not as opposites or contradictories, as they are in the eighth chapter of Romans, but as expressive of different degrees of spirituality, for the carnal believer is but a babe in Christ when he ought to be a grown man.

Every one must have observed that there are very great differences among Christians—differences of graces and gifts, and differences of degrees in these graces and gifts. Nay, more, there are great differences in the very same Christian at different periods of his life. His love, his confidence, his zeal, his devotion, his spirituality, are not always the same in degree or manifestation. Hence it is that sincere but thoughtless Christians, in ignorance or forgetfulness of these facts, often pass harsh judgments upon their fellow-Christians, even going so far as to class them with impenitent believers. Utterly failing to make due allowance for differences among Christians and for variations of spiritual life at different times in the same man, they do not hesitate with the utmost confidence and self-assertion to denounce as hypocrites those who are in deed and in truth their brethren in the Lord. If a believer is deficient in certain graces, or if in some hour of sore temptation, under the assaults of the devil, he falls into sin, these censorious persons at once proclaim that such a one is not a Christian; unmindful, apparently, of the fact that this rule of judg-

THE GROWTH OF FAITH. 89

ment, if applied to the lives of those we know were saints, would exclude Noah, Abraham, Moses, David and Peter from the blessed presence of God in heaven.

Faith, in its working, most marvelously develops the new life, increasing the believer's confidence in Christ and making the new man strong in the Lord, and enabling him, like a tree planted by rivers of water, to bring forth all the fruits of the Spirit in due season. The believer's confidence in Christ should increase from day to day; as he learns more of his blessed Lord he should rely more confidently on his faithful word. True, he may not at all times be conscious of this growth; nevertheless, it is certain that He who has begun a good work in him will carry it on unto completeness. The trees are not dead in the winter, though stripped of foliage; beneath the surface of the earth the roots are striking deeper and growing stronger. So with the trees in the garden of the Lord: there is growth, though unseen and unnoticed.

This increasing confidence in Christ, this growing faith in God, is manifested in the lives of all the saints. Nowhere do we find a more illustrious exemplification of this than in the life of Abraham, the Father of the Faithful. When the command of God came to him, "Get thee out of the country, and from thy kindred, and from thy father's house, unto a land that I will show thee," he "obeyed and went out, not knowing whither he went. By faith he sojourned in the land of promise as in a strange country, dwelling in tabernacles with Isaac and Jacob, the heirs with him of the same promise." In all this wandering his faith in God grew stronger and stronger, until at the divine command he took his beloved son Isaac, in whom all the Messianic hopes and promises centred, and prepared to offer him a burnt sacrifice on Mount Moriah. Then came the word of the Lord and his wondrous testimony to the power and manifestation of Abraham's faith: "Lay not thine hand upon the lad,

THE GROWTH OF FAITH. 91

neither do thou anything unto him; for now I know that thou fearest God, seeing thou hast not withheld thy son, thine only son, from me." His faith had been growing by exercise in all the years of his pilgrim-wanderings until it had reached such robust maturity that it staggered not at any command or promise of God, and was fully persuaded that God was abundantly able to keep, and would fully perform, all his promises.

As God leads his children along in their journey to the better country he wishes to have their filial confidence and love, and they must learn to walk by faith, not by sight; and just in proportion as God's children walk in simple faith in their heavenly Father and learn more of his tender mercy and loving care, the greater will be their confidence in him. In no one instance has God ever disappointed the confidence of any of his children. Almost every one has had some noble, generous, large-hearted friend in whom he confided, and as the years have gone by, and that friend has become better known, as more of his integrity and courage and tenderness and fidelity and love to man and God have been seen, confidence in him has continued to grow stronger and stronger. So with the Christian and his Saviour. As the believer follows on to know the Lord—to know him in all the depths and heights of his eternal love, and in all the matchless and marvelous tenderness of his human sympathy, having trusted and tried his Saviour a thousand times, and having never once found him to fail—his confidence becomes rooted as the everlasting hills, and no storm of earth nor blast from hell can shake it. Then with Paul he can say, "I know whom I have believed," and "I am persuaded, that neither death, nor life, nor angels, nor principalities, nor powers, nor things present, nor things to come, nor height, nor depth, nor any other creature, shall be able to separate us from the love of God, which is in Christ Jesus our Lord."

SECTION XI.

THE TRIALS OF FAITH.

THE trials of faith are most intimately and directly connected with its growth. The apostle Peter says to the elect of God, "That the trial of your faith, being much more precious than of gold that perisheth, though it be tried with fire, might be found unto praise and honor and glory at the appearing of Jesus Christ." The saints, "elect according to the foreknowledge of God the Father, through sanctification of the Spirit, unto obedience and sprinkling of the blood of Jesus Christ," and "begotten again to a lively hope," were "kept by the power of God through faith unto salvation." There was a needs-be that they should be "in heaviness through manifold temptations" of their faith, but this trial was most precious to them, and would also be to the honor of Jesus Christ at his appearing in his kingdom. God not only tried the faith of his friend Abraham, but he also tries the faith of all those who are the spiritual seed of Abraham and heirs according to the promise.

A devout student of Scripture writes thus: "Faith has its trials as well as its answers. It is not to be imagined that the man of faith, having pushed out from the shore of circumstances, finds it all smooth and easy sailing. By no means. Again and again he is called to encounter rough seas and stormy skies, but it is all graciously designed to lead him into deeper and more matured experience of what God is to the heart that confides in him. Were the sky always without a cloud and the ocean without a ripple, the believer would not know so well the God with whom he has to do; for, alas! we know how prone the heart is to mistake the peace of circumstances for the peace of God. When everything is going on smoothly and pleasantly, our property safe, our business prosperous, our children and servants carrying themselves agreeably, our residence comfortable, our health excellent—everything, in short, just to our mind—how apt we are to mistake the peace which reposes upon such circumstances for that peace which flows from the realized presence of Christ! The Lord knows this, and therefore he comes in one way and another and stirs up the nest—that is, if we are found nestling in circumstances instead of himself."

The whole word of God is the proper object of the believer's faith; he should esteem every word of God as precious. Just here many Christians are sadly at fault. They are disposed to regard certain portions of the divine word as more sure and steadfast than others, some of God's promises as more precious and certain of fulfillment than others, some truths revealed by him more credible than others. But if the faith of the believer is to stand, not in the wisdom of men, but in the power of God, then it is manifest that every truth revealed and every promise made by God is equally and alike steadfast and certain; not one jot or tittle can ever fail.

True faith receives the testimony of God upon his simple word as a Being of infinite truth who cannot lie. This is a wholly different thing from receiving the testimony of God because it corresponds with our preconceived views of what he ought to say and do; this is to find the foundations of faith, not in the infallible God, but in the finite reason. The devil has deceived many an unwary Christian on this very point. Christians sometimes use such language as the following: "I do not believe that such a doctrine is taught in the Bible; and if it is, I will reject the Bible." What the objectionable doctrine is, is of no consequence just now: the mistake and the sin are in saying, "I will reject the word of God if it teaches this doctrine." And this is gross unbelief in God, and a most heinous offence. So one condemns and rejects

THE TRIALS OF FAITH. 97

the word of God because it teaches the doctrine of election; another, because it teaches the supreme Godhead of Christ; another, because it authorizes the use, at the Lord's Supper, of wine that, if taken in excess, will intoxicate; another, because it does not specifically condemn this or that sin; and so on through the entire list of doctrines that are distasteful to the depraved heart of man. If we believe that the Bible contains the revealed will of God to man, who is he that will thus dare reject the teachings of infinite Wisdom because they do not accord with finite views of what God ought to teach?

In every age of the Church, God has tried the faith of his people by demanding of them implicit confidence in his word in spite of its seeming severity or of the impossibility of its accomplishment. He has been teaching his children the lesson that their Father in heaven was far more worthy of their confidence than anyone else or than all else in the boundless universe. Whatever the hindrances or difficulties or obstacles in the way of his word, he, their Father God, was above and superior to them all, and his word would surely come to pass.

The testimony of God that tries the faith of his saints has respect sometimes to the past, at other times to the present, and at yet other times to the future; and in the Scriptures we have most signal illustrations of how the confidence of God's children in their heavenly Father triumphed gloriously over all the difficulties of sight and of sense.

Consider how severely the faith of Noah, the hero of the antediluvian world, was tried. To him God revealed his purpose to destroy the race by the waters of a flood, commanding him to build an ark for the saving of himself and his house. During the hundred and twenty years in which God waited with a wicked world the faith of Noah was on trial. Doubtless the scientists of that age demonstrated to the entire satisfaction of the whole unbelieving world that such a flood as

THE TRIALS OF FAITH. 99

Noah's God had threatened was a scientific impossibility. These men, wise in their own conceit, may have reasoned thus—just as the men of our day reason: "This flood can never come to pass; Nature is fixed and uniform in all her operations. The land and the water are separated by indestructible barriers. Nature never acts contrary to her own established order. Since the days of Adam the windows of heaven have been closed, and there has been no rain, nor any catastrophe of any sort, upon the earth, and such a flood as the one that is threatened is contrary to the universal experience of men, and is not only impossible, but is incredible even in thought. All things will continue as they have been from the first; there will be in the future, as there have been in the past, evolution and development, but no flood caused by the will and the power of a personal God." So the cultured scientific thought of that day gave no heed to the word of the living God, and the flood came and swept the world away.

Noah believed God, obeyed the divine command, built the ark to the saving of his house, and became heir of the righteousness which is by faith. What a trial it must have been to him that of all his fellow-men on the earth not even one thought and believed as he did! We can hold to our beliefs with much greater tenacity when we know that multitudes cling to them in common with ourselves; it tests the strength and the steadfastness of a faith when we hold it singly and alone. In this instance one man clings to his confidence in God with the whole world against him. The true ark-builders of God have been in every age an infinitesimal minority of the human race.

Both the Old and the New Testament make special mention of the trial of Abraham's faith, and, in fact, his entire life was most signally marked with trials of his confidence in his covenant God. Omitting any mention of the minor trials of his faith, let us fix our attention on that great test which God himself appointed, and the triumphant endurance of which justly entitles him to be called "the Father of the Faithful:" "It came to pass that God did tempt (try) Abraham; and said unto him, Take now thy son, thine only son Isaac, whom thou lovest, and get thee unto the land of Moriah; and offer him there for a burnt offering, upon one of the mountains which I will tell thee of." This man might have argued that this command was contrary to the very nature which God himself had given him, that it would be a most unnatural murder to slay his only son, that it would be subversive of the covenant promises of God, that it was in direct conflict with the law of God, and that it would prove destructive of the covenant of grace which God had made with him, and wherein all the nations of the earth were to be blessed; yet so implicit was the confidence of the patriarch in his covenant-keeping God that he did not hesitate for a single moment to obey the divine command. He staggered not at the word of the Lord, but, accounting that God was able to raise his son from the dead, strong in faith he promptly obeyed, giving glory to God. Having thus passed sublimely through the fiery ordeal, he had this testimony borne to him by the Lord himself: "Now I know that thou fearest God, seeing thou hast not withheld thy son, thine only son, from me."

Sometimes God tries the faith of his saints by commanding them to do some apparently impossible thing, of which the command to Joshua and Israel to capture Jericho affords a most notable illustration. Jericho was a strongly-fortified and walled city, the key to the Land of Canaan. Joshua and the children of Israel were commanded to compass the city seven days, the priests going before the ark of the covenant and blowing upon trumpets of rams' horns. On the seventh day they were to compass the city seven times, the priests to make a long blast with the rams' horns and the people to give a great shout, and the promise was that the walls of the city should fall down flat. The Jericho generals doubtless laughed at the simplicity of Joshua's faith, and showed conclusively that since the creation of the world the walls of no city had ever been thrown down in this way, and that the entire procedure was a military absurdity; and if there had been no living personal God in Israel's camp, the Jericho generals would have been right in their conclusions. But Joshua's faith in this present God was stronger than anything and everything else besides; he obeyed the divine command because he believed the divine promise. The priests blew the horns, the people gave the shout, the walls fell flat and the city was captured.

In the case of Noah, faith led him, upon the simple word of God, to prepare for an event far in the future which the whole world declared to be impossible; in the case of Abraham, faith enabled him, at the divine command, to yield up to God what was far dearer to him than life; in the case of Joshua, faith led him to capture a great and walled city with instrumentalities which of themselves were wholly insufficient for the work. By faith Noah prepared the ark, by faith Abraham offered up Isaac, by faith the walls of Jericho fell down; and in each instance the faith that so gloriously triumphed was severely tried.

Faith's trial has not yet ended, nor will it end until the Lord himself shall descend in glory from the skies. Nor should any believer suppose, when his faith is tried, that some strange thing has happened to him: his life from its beginning to its end is a walk with God by faith. The language of his heart ought to be —

"So I go on, not knowing;
  I would not if I might:
It is better to walk in the dark with God
  Than walk alone in the light."

Every hope that we cherish concerning the life that lies beyond the grave is derived from the word of God; apart from that we have no knowledge whatever of that infinite and eternal future to which we are so rapidly and surely hastening, nor of that glorious and blessed life that stretches boundlessly away into the unending ages. As it is by faith we understand that the worlds were framed by the word of God, so also it is by faith that we know of the resurrection of the body, the heavenly recognition and reunion, the fullness of those joys that are at his right hand and the pleasures that are for evermore; and yet the believer's faith is the substance of all these hoped-for things and the perfectly-satisfying evidence of these certain and imperishable realities.

Now, as heretofore, the believer's faith is often tried; fears arise, doubts distress, Satan assails, confidence falters, and the sorely-tempted child of God is brought to the brink of despair. But the very trial drives him closer to God to take refuge in the everlasting loving arms of his heavenly Father, and there in peace and safety his soul doth abide until the calamities are overpast. The patriarch Jacob, even when he had God's promise in his hand and heart, cried out in anguish, "All these things are against me;" and since then thousands of the saints, as the waves and deep billows have gone over them, have lifted up the same sad cry: "All these things are against me;" yet not one has failed to find that under the all-controlling providence of God all these things were working together for his good.

How sorely is faith tried when disease fastens on the frame, when the days grow into weeks, the weeks into months, the months into years; when sharp and grinding poverty enters the home, and the wife wants raiment, and the children cry for bread; when death comes and lays his hand upon the loved one's heart and there is a vacant seat, an absent form, a "vanished hand;" when Jacob exclaims, "Me have ye bereft of my children;" when Rachel weeps for her dead and cannot be comforted! Thrice blessed is the man who at such times can rest with unwavering confidence in the sure mercies of his Father in heaven, and who rejoices in his Saviour God who giveth songs in the night. But through trials and tribulations, through storms and tempests, through darkness and distress, faith moves steadily on to its final triumph and eternal consummation in glory: "Whatsoever is born of God overcometh the world; and this is the victory that overcometh the world, even our faith."

In this world, and of it a part, we are under the curse, in the power of the devil and under sentence of death, and, dying, we must get the victory over it and get out of it into a realm of life or else perish for ever. Christ has conquered in our place and for us; he has gotten the victory over sin, death and the devil. Faith unites us to him, lifts us out of the sphere of death into that of life, unites us as living members to our living Head, and so in him we also win the victory, and are brought off more than conquerors.

Begotten and born of God, walking by faith in the unseen, and not by sight in the seen, living lives of faith upon the Son of God, we too overcome the world, the lust of the flesh, the lust of the eyes and the pride of life, and the victory that overcomes this world is our faith. Blessed are they that have not seen, and yet have believed!

THE END.

www.ingramcontent.com/pod-product-compliance
Lightning Source LLC
Chambersburg PA
CBHW030907170426
43193CB00009BA/758